Becoming a Successful and Outstanding Auto Broker

Learn how to sell cars by employing strategic ideas, and create lasting impact in the automotive industry and beyond, through your business

ANTHONY AFACHUNG

Dedication

I dedicate this book to the source of life, who speaks and brings forth reality. Whose word penetrates barriers, whose word is a double-edged sword, healing the sick and restoring lost years. To the One who completes me, whose I am, who orchestrates my being, and who will illuminate the readers of this book to envision boundless possibilities, shattering mental constraints, and flourishing in all pursuits.

To the one true God, his son Jesus Christ seated at his right hand, and the gentle Holy Spirit who resides within us.

May God's kingdom reign eternally, blessing its builders, and may we persist in constructing through prayer, worship, and the fulfilment of God's will with our hands.

May the earth be filled with the knowledge of the glory of God, His love, and His willingness to help everyone He has formed, for as many that call on His name shall be saved. In Jesus' name, Amen.

Acknowledgement

I gratefully acknowledge God, who causes me to flourish like grains and blossom like grapevines, causing me to be as fragrant as the wines of Lebanon, making my feet swift and my hands skilled for battle. Bless the name of God, all the earth.

I am grateful to my parents, Dr. Pius and Dr. Oluwatoyin Afachung, for providing me with a quality education, establishing moral foundations and affection for society, and to my siblings, Julia and Kennedy, whose companionship brings peace and sanity. My love for my family knows no bounds.

Special thanks to my childhood friend, Okechukwu Chibueze, for his invaluable editing contributions. Chiboy, envision my gratitude in a warm embrace every time you read this.

I must also express my appreciation to my cousin, Mercy Ogedengbe, a talented graphics artist who assisted with editing the book cover. Mercy, you are truly exceptional, and may God bless you abundantly.

To every diligent worker, every kingdom builder, and every child of God, I urge you: do not falter, for God is near. He will establish you and your endeavours. Wait upon Him and continue to rely on His unfailing grace. As Psalm 138:8 assures us, His enduring love will fulfil God's plan for your life, and He will never forsake you. May your strength be renewed, your mind expanded to perceive God's possibilities, and your subconscious made receptive to His light and presence, enabling you to rise and shine in every aspect of your life. In Jesus' name, Amen.

Table of Contents

Chapter 1: The Profound Role of an Auto Broker

In the intricate world of automobiles, akin to how stockbrokers master stocks and insurance brokers navigate the intricacies of insurance, auto brokers possess unparalleled car expertise. Also known as car brokers, these automotive professionals, often with a sales background, provide a unique service to car buyers. Their role involves

- Sourcing and negotiating car deals on behalf of the buyer.
- Streamlining the often-complex process.
- Leaving the final decision to the buyer.

Navigating the Process as an Auto Broker

Potential clients seek the expertise of an auto broker, often without a clear idea of what they want but with the shared goal of identifying quality cars and securing favourable deals. The beauty of becoming an auto broker lies in its accessibility; anyone with genuine interest, passion, and a commitment to continuous learning and hard work can embark on this journey. This guide has been crafted to assist those aspiring to get into this field, providing insights to help build a successful career that is both financially rewarding and impactful.

Commencing the Journey

The initial step involves identifying a reputable auto broker with positive reviews and a proven track record. The engagement often begins with a nominal retainer, typically around $100 or less, considering factors such as the client's relationship, business size, and other relevant considerations. This initial financial commitment serves as a symbolic gesture of dedication.

Navigating Client Preferences

As an auto broker, maintaining a delicate balance is critical—being patient and proactive while assisting clients in understanding their preferences. This process is integral to collecting detailed information that guides the search for the ideal car. The ability to patiently navigate through client preferences ensures a comprehensive understanding, streamlining the subsequent search process.

Meticulous Car Search

Following the establishment of clear client preferences, the auto broker meticulously searches for a car that aligns with these criteria. The depth of detail the client provides significantly influences the presentation of options that closely resonate with their preferences. A transparent and comprehensive communication process expedites the search, resulting in a more satisfying outcome.

Payment Structure

The discussion around payment is a crucial aspect for auto brokers. Various fee structures can be explored, including a flat fee or a percentage based on the purchase price versus the car's value. Typically, fees for used cars are higher due to the additional effort required to source specific models. Opting for a percentage model ties the broker's compensation directly to the amount saved, creating a financial incentive for skilled negotiation, and securing favourable prices.

In essence, the journey of an auto broker is a dynamic interplay of client engagement, meticulous search processes, and thoughtful fee structures. This profession opens doors to financial success and allows individuals to make a positive impact by guiding clients towards fulfilling automotive experiences.

Benefits of Engaging a Car Broker

Despite the intuitive hesitation to involve an intermediary in the car-buying process, the tangible benefits of working with car brokers are significant.

1. **Financial Savings:** Unlike expectations, engaging a broker almost always leads to substantial financial savings. Leveraging their insider knowledge of the industry, brokers secure deals that surpass what an individual buyer could negotiate independently. The significant savings obtained make the broker's fees reasonable.
2. **Locating the Perfect Car:** The expertise of a car broker shines in the pursuit of the perfect car. Unlike individual buyers, who might compromise on certain aspects due to limited options, brokers excel at precisely identifying what clients want. Their ability to find unique, special-edition or rare vehicles sets them apart from traditional dealership experiences.
3. **Time Efficiency:** An invaluable aspect of engaging a broker is the time saved. Drawing on their extensive experience, brokers efficiently navigate potential sources, eliminating the need for exhaustive exploration. This time efficiency is especially beneficial for individuals with constraints on time and energy.
4. **Reduced Stress (Dealing with Salespeople):** Dealing with salespeople can be extremely stressful. Auto brokers shield buyers from the intricate sales tactics employed by dealership staff. Their familiarity with these tactics ensures a smoother experience, allowing you to focus on the final decision without unnecessary stress.
5. **Brokers Work for Clients:** A fundamental distinction lies in the fact that car brokers work for clients, i.e., the car buyer, not the dealership. Their commitment to securing the best possible deal aligns with their professional reputation. However, buyers should remain vigilant for signs of undue influence, ensuring the broker truly represents their interests.

In essence, the role of an auto broker goes beyond what you traditionally know, offering a profound and indispensable service that transforms the car-buying experience into a streamlined, efficient, and financially advantageous endeavour.

Setting Fees as an Auto Broker: A Professional Approach

As you establish your auto broker business, treating it with the professionalism it deserves is paramount. Working without compensation is unsustainable, and instances of clients taking advantage of relationships underline the necessity for a transparent and fair payment structure.

Key Recommendations:

1. **Formalise Agreements with Contracts:**
   - Create a written contract to formalise the engagement, signed by all parties.
   - Ensure the contract is in line with or attuned to the specific laws and regulations of the country and state.
   - Avoid mediocrity by clearly outlining roles, expectations, and the agreed-upon commission.
   - Ensure compliance with registration requirements to execute legally binding contracts.
2. **Essential Contract Components:**
   - Define the roles of each party in the transaction or business.
   - State expectations to avoid misunderstandings.
   - Outline the commission structure comprehensively.
3. **Legal Recognition:**
   - Once signed, the contract becomes a legally recognised agreement under state or country laws.

Factors Influencing Fee Structure

1. **Relationship with the Client:** The nature and depth of your relationship with the client play a pivotal role in determining the fee structure. For long-standing clients or those who consistently bring business, you might be more flexible or offer discounted rates as a gesture of appreciation. On the other hand, new clients or one-time transactions may warrant a standard fee.
2. **The extent of work involved:** It's crucial to thoroughly evaluate the complexity and volume of work required for each transaction. More intricate deals, extensive negotiations, or additional services such as market research or legal documentation will naturally demand a higher fee. Clearly defining the scope of work helps justify your charges and avoids misunderstandings.
3. **Geographical Location:** The geographical location of the transaction can influence the fee structure. In regions with higher living costs or where the demand for your services is greater, you may be justified in charging higher fees. Conversely, a more moderate fee structure may be appropriate in less competitive markets, where clients might be more price-sensitive.

4. **Client's Preferences:** Considering your client's preferences and requirements is crucial. Some clients may prefer a flat fee for budgeting purposes, while others may appreciate the transparency of a percentage-based model. Flexibility in accommodating client preferences can contribute to a positive working relationship.

You may be perturbed about what pricing tool to use, especially after considering a factor determining your price. Using a flat fee or a percentage-based method is entirely up to you, but let your conclusion be guided by careful consideration. See below as we lay bare the two methods.

Flat Fee vs. Percentage-Based

Choosing between a flat fee and a percentage-based model is a critical decision. A flat fee provides predictability for both you and the client, but it may not always reflect the true value of your services. On the other hand, a percentage-based model aligns your compensation with the success of the transaction, demonstrating a shared interest in achieving the best outcome.

I recommend a percentage-based model (Please note that this is only a recommendation; you are advised to apply whatever legal and suitable pricing methods work best for you)

In my own opinion, after careful thinking and application, here are a few reasons I recommend using percentage based charging;

1. **Consistency in Approach:** Adopting a percentage-based fee structure ensures consistency in your pricing approach. It establishes a fair and proportional link between your compensation and the value of the transaction, irrespective of its size or complexity.
2. **Professionalism:** A percentage-based model signals professionalism to clients. It conveys that your fees are not arbitrary but based on industry standards and the value you bring to the table. This can enhance your perceived expertise and trustworthiness.
3. **Alignment with Industry Standards:** Charging a percentage aligns your fee structure with industry standards and expectations. This alignment reinforces the idea that your pricing is fair and in line with what is commonly accepted in the auto brokerage industry.
4. **Deserving Fair Compensation:** The percentage-based approach reinforces the principle that your expertise deserves fair compensation. It communicates that you are invested in the success of the transaction and that your remuneration is directly tied to the results you achieve for your clients.

By choosing a percentage-based fee structure, you create a more transparent and equitable pricing model and position yourself as a professional auto broker committed to delivering value. This approach helps build trust, fosters long-term client relationships, and establishes your credibility within the industry.

QUESTIONS AND REFLECTIONS

1. Consider your own experiences with purchasing a car. How much do you value your time in the car-buying process? Could the engagement of an auto broker have made the process more efficient and stress-free?
2. In your opinion, how can an auto broker's expertise contribute to a car buyer's financial savings? Can you envision scenarios where their insider knowledge might secure deals that an individual buyer could not achieve independently?
3. The chapter discusses the benefits of engaging a car broker, including financial savings, locating the perfect car, time efficiency, and reduced stress. Reflect on which of these benefits resonates with you the most and why.
4. The chapter emphasises the need for a system and a structure in the auto brokerage business. How can implementing a systematic approach contribute to enduring success in this field? What challenges might arise without a structured system?
5. Consider the factors influencing the fee structure mentioned in the chapter, such as the relationship with the client, the extent of work involved, geographical location, and client preferences. How would you weigh these factors when determining your own fee structure as an auto broker?
6. The chapter recommends a percentage-based charging approach. Do you agree with this recommendation, and why? How might adopting a percentage-based model align with industry standards and enhance professionalism?
7. What are the advantages and disadvantages of a flat fee versus a percentage-based fee structure for auto brokers? How might each model impact the perceived value of the services provided?

Chapter 2: 12 Practical Steps to Take to Become a Successful and Outstanding Auto Broker.

Why would someone discuss achieving success and being outstanding? That's because they are the same. The reason is straightforward: they are distinct concepts. Attaining success may be relatively straightforward—a few steps and you're there—but standing out requires more. It demands grit, determination, sacrifice, time, resources, and consistency. It's a higher standard to meet, which is precisely what this book aims to help my readers achieve in the auto brokerage industry.

In pursuing any goal, some pathways could lead to success, and some should be taken unequivocally for assured progress. The latter is paramount in becoming a successful auto broker. It surpasses the traces of excitement, possibly the anxiety and impatience found in gestures like designing a logo or establishing a social media presence. True success in this field hinges on authenticity—a quality that cannot be bought. In this chapter, you will learn the twelve foundational steps that foster authenticity and pave the way for enduring success in the auto brokerage business. While not everyone may initially possess the total capacity to embark on this journey, each step taken is a stride towards expanding one's potential. Take it one step at a time, and witness how your mindset expands to embrace unforeseen possibilities with each progressive effort.

1. The Blueprint for Auto Brokerage Success - Early Commitment and Strategic Focus

Becoming a thriving auto broker transcends mere enthusiasm; it demands a considered strategy and an unwavering commitment to acquiring a profound understanding of the industry. The critical foundation for success lies in getting serious early in your pursuit of excellence in auto brokerage. Passion is the driving force, but strategic intent propels you forward. Moving beyond passion involves recognising that more than passion alone will be required. It requires a deliberate immersion into the complex world of auto brokering. Understand that the path to success demands more than surface-level enthusiasm; it demands a proactive approach to gaining in-depth knowledge.

The first crucial step is to understand the nuances of the business. Merge your passion with a thirst for knowledge. Be intentional in connecting with seasoned professionals who have walked the path before you. Approach this stage with modesty, recognising that learning from the experiences of others is a powerful accelerator for your growth.

In the initial stages, the art of being observant is transformative. While passion fuels your journey, a certain level of discretion allows you to observe and absorb insights without unnecessary distractions. Networking is vital, but in your interactions, balance speaking and listening. This intentional quietness becomes a tool for focused strategizing. You can listen intently and generate purposeful questions to ask if you have any.

Networking is the lifeblood of success in auto brokerage. Connect with reputable car sellers, engage with industry peers on social media platforms, and stay attuned to the dynamic trends within the field.

Seriousness extends beyond passion and knowledge to the formalities of business. Registering your auto brokering venture and adhering to the country's policies are non-negotiable steps. Treating your endeavour as a legitimate business from the outset establishes the foundation for a professional and service-oriented approach, setting the stage for sustained success. Unravelling the layers of getting serious early in your journey to becoming a successful auto broker involves the strategic onset, blending passion with knowledge, the power of intent observation, networking dynamics, and the formalities of success.

2. Beyond Profit: Delivering Quality Service for Lasting Impact

While the pursuit of financial success is a natural inclination, the essence of a successful auto broker surpasses monetary gains. An integral aspect of achieving longevity and recognition is delivering unparalleled quality service. Striking a balance between profitability and service excellence is the key to a thriving auto brokerage venture.

The business's true beauty lies in its impact on clients' lives. Imagine being celebrated globally for providing the best auto service or service in any industry. Imagine families expressing gratitude for the car purchased, the GPS tracker installed, or the engine expertly fixed. Beyond the transactional nature of the business, the joy of contributing positively to clients' lives becomes a motivating force.

In this step, we delve into the mindset shift required to view the auto brokering profession as a means to financial success and a platform for making a genuine difference. The narrative explores the fulfilment and happiness derived from delivering top-notch service. Building a reputation for diligence and a commitment to excellence sets the stage for a lasting legacy and a flourishing auto brokering career.

3. The Power of Automotive Knowledge - Elevating Your Auto Brokerage Prowess

In exploring elevating your prowess in the auto brokerage industry, we delve into a fundamental principle: the imperative need for comprehensive automotive knowledge. Understanding cars, their brands, and the mechanisms driving the automotive world forms the backbone of success in this field.

Possessing an in-depth understanding of cars is not merely a bonus but a necessity for auto brokers. Your commitment to knowing cars inside out should be unwavering. This includes familiarity with specific models and the nuances of their construction, functionalities, and the driving force behind their designs.

To navigate the diverse landscape of auto brokerage, it is essential to understand the diversity of car brands. Basic knowledge about brands such as Lexus, a Toyota or Chevrolet creation representing U.S. craftsmanship, is crucial for unlocking proficiency in the field. Familiarising yourself with different brands' unique characteristics and market positions is indispensable.

A grasp of the essential functions of a car is non-negotiable for anyone entering the auto business. Understanding how different car components work, from engines to transmissions, enhances confidence in the sales world. Clients place their trust in your expertise, which becomes a catalyst for referrals and sustained success.

Foundational and growing knowledge about cars and car brands across various countries becomes a powerful asset. This knowledge is not just about impressing clients; it's about exuding confidence in the sales world. As a consultant, your clients rely on your expertise to make informed decisions. The more confident and knowledgeable you are, the more trust you inspire.

Clients who engage in your services benefit from your expertise and become ambassadors for your business. The trust you instil in them transforms them into advocates, referring your services to others. Your reputation as someone too good to be ignored becomes the driving force behind organic business growth.

In the ever-evolving automotive landscape, pursuing knowledge is a continuous journey. Commit to constant learning about new car models, emerging technologies, and shifts in market trends. This ongoing commitment to staying informed positions you as a dynamic and invaluable player in the auto brokerage industry.

4. Mastering Your Finances - The Unyielding Power of Financial Discipline

In the dynamic realm of auto brokerage, success hinges on a passion for service and fiscal acumen, where financial discipline emerges as a pivotal key to lasting prosperity. We underscore the importance of financial knowledge and discipline, illuminating the path towards strategic monetary management within the auto brokerage business.

Amidst the skills and traits at your disposal, financial knowledge and discipline stand as non-negotiable pillars for any successful businessperson. Mastering money's workings and the ability to wield financial strategies with precision have become indispensable tools in the auto brokerage journey.

Understanding how money works is not merely a suggestion; it's an imperative. This involves a subtle comprehension of the flow of money within your business, the art of reinvestment, and the strategic utilisation of financial resources. The discernment to refuse instant gratification and instead focus on long-term gains becomes a hallmark of financial wisdom.

When considering equipment or cutting-edge technology purchases, a thorough evaluation is critical. Assess the utility and value of each acquisition within the context of your business. Strategic decision-making involves weighing the benefits against the costs, ensuring that each financial move aligns with the overarching goals of your auto brokerage venture.

Defining your compensation structure requires understanding how much to pay yourself and others. Are you adopting a percentage-based principle, or do you have a customised system in place? Seeking the expertise of a finance professional becomes imperative to establishing a fair and sustainable payment framework.

Navigating the complex waters of financial discipline often necessitates the guidance of experts. Engaging a finance professional can provide invaluable insights. These experts, who dedicate their lives to imparting financial wisdom, can guide you in making informed financial decisions tailored to the nuances of the auto brokerage industry.

In pursuing financial discipline, mastering the balance between saving, investing, and philanthropy becomes paramount. Learn how to allocate resources for the growth of your business, wisely invest for future ventures, and discern the extent of philanthropic endeavours your business can afford in a given financial year.

5. The Art and Essence of Selling - Transforming Potential into Prosperity

The ability to sell isn't merely a chore or responsibility; it's an essential skill that forms the bedrock of success. This step delves into the profound art of selling, highlighting its transformative potential and pivotal role in propelling your auto brokerage venture to new heights.

Reimagine selling not as a task but as a fundamental skill you must possess. You have a voice, a brain that works, and a beautifully active mind—all the tools necessary to master the art of selling. It's not about coercion; it's about compellingly conveying the value of your products or services.

Your brain serves as your first and most potent tool in the art of selling. Strategic thinking lies at the core of effective salesmanship. Reflect on your unique value proposition, understand your customer's needs, and employ well-thought-out strategies to connect the dots between what you offer and what your customers desire.

A personal anecdote illustrates the simplicity of marketing: convincing people to buy what you sell. While marketing may encompass elaborate strategies, at its core, it's about connecting with people and compelling them to purchase. Simplifying this concept highlights the importance of clear communication and understanding your audience.

Selling is not a one-time skill but a continuous process of development. You'll encounter diverse people, cultures, and nations as an auto broker. Adapting your selling strategies to resonate with different audiences is very necessary. Continuous development involves honing skills in various areas, from languages to content creation and public speaking.

Consider the multifaceted nature of selling. If English proficiency is essential, learn it. If content creation enhances your selling strategy, invest time in mastering it. Public speaking is another valuable skill that can elevate your ability to connect with clients. Whatever skills you need to enhance your sales, embark on a journey of learning and implementation.

Embarking on the sales journey may seem daunting, but every expert starts somewhere. Begin with the skills you currently possess and incrementally work on enhancing them as you grow. Whether it's language proficiency, content creation, or public speaking, each step contributes to your development as a proficient auto broker.

6. Catalysing Transformation - The Power of Diversification

Diversification emerges as a potent catalyst for transformative growth. This concept goes beyond conventional boundaries, aiming for wealth accumulation and meaningful contributions to societal challenges.

Contentment can be deceiving. While some may profess satisfaction, there's an argument that there's always more to be done, not just for wealth but for addressing the world's multifaceted problems. It's a call to challenge the status quo and think beyond the ordinary.

Think about the ripple effect of your auto brokerage beyond mere transactions. Imagine the lives you could impact and the positive contributions your business could make to society. Diversification becomes a tool for extending your influence and leaving a lasting legacy.

Pause and acknowledge the societal issues around us. Recognise the honesty in admitting the global problems, from unemployment to environmental concerns. Let these realities fuel your motivation for meaningful change through diversification.

Corporate social responsibility should go beyond traditional notions. Consider how your business can positively impact society, from employing individuals to initiating charity programmes. Reflect on addressing regional challenges like hunger and education.

Start diversifying by identifying pain points in your environment. Think creatively about solutions, such as offering GPS tracking services or partnering with technicians for comprehensive servicing. Explore retailing auto parts and providing education in car maintenance.

Look beyond transactions to create lasting impacts. Whether setting up a car wash or partnering with educational institutions, innovate and solve pain points while leaving a significant mark on your community and beyond.

7. Expand Your Business Horizon: Navigating the Path to Global Recognition

Success transcends familiar boundaries. Extending operations beyond accustomed territories is essential for true thriving in this field. This journey involves recognising the need for expansion and venturing into new territories. Even if the expansion strategy isn't immediately clear, initiating the process is crucial.

Engaging with potential customers beyond current regions is a strategic move. Thorough market research helps understand the preferences and needs of diverse audiences. We leverage digital platforms, social media, and targeted marketing aids to reach untapped markets. Establishing a presence in new regions is about more than just boosting sales and building brand recognition and trust.

Expanding promotional efforts by advertising in neighbouring regions and beyond is vital. Crafting culturally resonant campaigns and collaborating with local influencers enhance credibility and create personalised connections with potential customers. Effective advertising can make your brand a compelling force that attracts customers.

Expanding operations necessitates readiness for change. Embracing the dynamic nature of the auto brokerage industry and adjusting strategies based on market demands is crucial. Flexibility and adaptability are paramount when navigating unfamiliar territories. Anticipating challenges, learning from them, and refining approaches are essential.

Achieving growth in various regions demonstrates the transformative effects of a global presence. Connecting with diverse clients and meeting their automotive needs adds depth to your venture beyond financial success.

This step emphasises practical steps for expansion, highlighting strategic outreach, cultural sensitivity in advertising, and the transformative effects of a global presence. Expanding your business horizons broadens opportunities and positions you as an important player in the evolving landscape of auto brokerage.

8. Riding the Wave of Innovation - Navigating Trends and Technologies in Auto Brokerage

Staying ahead in the auto brokerage industry means more than merely understanding the present; it's about anticipating and embracing the future. Our world is rapidly evolving, particularly in terms of technology, and being attuned to these changes is not just advantageous but essential for success. Embracing the rapid pace of change positions your auto brokerage business to thrive in an environment where innovation is the driving force.

Artificial Intelligence (AI) is a monumental game-changer, offering transformative capabilities such as language transformation and personalised customer experiences. From chatbots to AI filters for data processing, AI opens avenues for enhancing customer interactions and operational efficiency.

Understanding how to leverage AI and other emerging technologies, whether establishing an online presence, utilising social media, or adopting AI solutions strategically, is crucial for sustained success. Discerning what works best for your business and avoiding unnecessary controversies arising from certain technological implementations is essential.

Continuous learning is paramount for sustainable growth in this dynamic landscape. As a businessperson, staying informed about the latest trends, technologies, and best practices empowers you to make informed decisions that contribute to the growth of your auto brokerage business.

In navigating the interplay of trends and technologies within auto brokerage, this step serves as a guide for harnessing the transformative power of AI, strategically adopting technologies, and prioritising continuous learning to stay ahead in the ever-evolving industry landscape.

9. Anticipating Evolution - Embracing Change for Business Growth

The ability to expect and embrace change becomes a cornerstone of sustained success. This step explores the necessity of anticipating change and adequately preparing for the transformative journey ahead.

Just as Newton's third law governs the natural world, the business world operates similarly. Every action you take in your auto brokerage venture will produce a reaction. This fundamental truth underscores the importance of expecting change as a natural part of the entrepreneurial journey. Just as you anticipate the car starting when you turn the ignition, foresee shifts and adaptations in your business environment.

After putting in the work and making the necessary sacrifices, the next step is preparing for the unforeseen. Drawing a parallel to a growing family contemplating additional children, expanding your business horizons requires foresight. Consider partnerships, branching out to new locations, or establishing outlet stores. As a family may contemplate a larger house or relocation, a business owner should envision growth through diversification.

While viewing an auto brokerage business as a simple venture might be tempting, true growth comes from a deeper understanding. Shifting the mindset from a narrow focus to one of expansive possibilities opens the door to significant business development. Like a family preparing for various changes with the arrival of children, an entrepreneur should contemplate potential shifts, such as partnerships, geographic expansions, and training staff.

Resisting the mindset that deems an auto business as "not that deep" is necessary to avoid stagnation. Little or no growth is often the outcome for companies that fail to consider the broader spectrum of possibilities. Visualise the potential changes—customers from different states or countries, government collaboration, educational institutions seeking your services, and many individuals relying on your expertise.

Establishing your business as an immovable rock in its core offerings is commendable, but considering yourself dispensable is a paradigm shift. To thrive in a dynamic market, think of diversification. Envision possibilities beyond the ordinary, such as exploring new customer bases, branching into different markets, and training a skilled workforce. This readiness for change positions your business as a reliable entity and a dynamic force poised for continual growth.

10. Upholding Integrity - The Pillars of Character in Auto Brokerage

The essence of character emerges as a foundational element that propels you forward and sustains your presence in the industry. Establishing and developing character is crucial for enduring success, emphasising virtues that serve as the bedrock of your journey.

Character serves as the sustainer of vision. While your initial vision or idea may have led you into the auto brokerage arena, character ensures longevity and continued success. This encompasses many qualities, including honesty, respect, foresight, diligence, and kindness. These attributes distinguish you in your interactions with customers, business partners, and staff, forming the cornerstone of your professional relationships.

Honesty stands as the cornerstone of trust. Committing to transparent dealings and interactions with all stakeholders in your auto brokerage venture builds trust beyond individual transactions. Being forthright about cars' condition, documentation, and potential issues fosters credibility and long-term relationships.

Respect forms the foundation of professional relationships. Treating people with respect—customers, business partners, or staff—carries immense significance. Honouring your word, delivering on promises, and providing quality goods and services prioritise long-term relationships over momentary gains, reflecting your character.

Foresight prevails over short-term gains. Resisting the allure of quick money, you focus on the potential and possibilities of the present and future. Transparency regarding a car's condition and guidance on necessary repairs contribute to building a reputation for trustworthiness, transcending individual transactions.

Diligence in client services is paramount. Exerting due diligence in your responsibilities, you invest your skills and efforts to fulfil client requests. Open communication and exploring alternatives in the face of challenges demonstrate your commitment to delivering the best service possible, defining your role as an auto broker and reinforcing your professional character.

Treating staff and partners with kindness is essential. Your demeanour toward your team and business partners reflects your character. Showing kindness in speech and action acknowledges their humanity and the shared responsibility to cultivate a positive work environment. Upholding a culture of respect and kindness contributes to your auto brokerage venture's overall success and sustainability.

11. Unveiling Unconventional Strategies - The Art of Meditative Business Thinking

In the vast expanse of the auto brokerage industry, where innovation is the currency of success, step 11 invites you to move past conventional thinking. Whether you're a 9-to-5er or a full-time entrepreneur, exploring uncommon strategies becomes a transformative journey.

Walking the field of the auto brokerage industry demands more than routine operations. It requires a willingness to delve into uncharted territories and uncover strategies that defy the ordinary. Whether contemplating building innovation or exploring partnerships, this step encourages you to think beyond the expected.

Meditation, in the context of business thinking, becomes a powerful tool for unlocking creative solutions. Whether you're a seasoned entrepreneur or just starting, dedicating time to reflect on your auto brokerage business allows you to tap into the depths of your creativity and envision pathways to extraordinary success.

Strategic partnerships emerge as a powerful tool in the quest for unconventional strategies. Engage with financing houses and loan providers to enhance customer accessibility. Partner with car enthusiasts, influencers, and brands to add depth and diversity to your initiatives. These collaborations can elevate your auto brokerage business and create a lasting impact.

The essence of this step lies in the art of business meditation—dedicating focused time to reflect on your business, ideate, and envision unconventional strategies. Embrace the notion that your mind is a treasure trove of innovative ideas waiting to be unearthed. Allocate moments during your days to meditate on your business, and you'll discover the extraordinary potential within.

12. God, the Divine Source - Acknowledging and Nurturing Spiritual Prosperity in Auto Brokerage

As we delve into the realm beyond conventional business wisdom, acknowledging God as the divine source that transcends human understanding, we invite you to consider the profound impact of incorporating spiritual principles into your auto brokerage journey.

In the aftermath of sermons or altar calls, it's customary to recognise God as the divine source—the giver of life and everything. For those who may not share this spiritual perspective, please continue sipping your tea. The acknowledgement here is rooted in the belief that a transcendent force is at play in our lives, and we can't live in folly and deny that God is our source.

The Bible, a revered text for many, declares that God is the provider of the power to accumulate wealth (Deuteronomy 8:18). This power encompasses strength, wisdom, health, favour, and the ability to conceive uncommon strategies for wealth creation. And we further gaze upon the light from Isaiah 48:17, where we see that God, our Redeemer, the Holy One of Israel Himself, teaches us to profit; he leads us by the way we should go. How could we not believe it, especially after discovering the frailty of man? Even our strength cannot save us, so we choose to think of the very word of God, which is true, spirit, and life itself. It's a holistic endowment that extends beyond material riches to encompass the essence of a prosperous life.

While the mention of God's blessings may resonate differently with each reader, the concept remains universal—acknowledging a force greater than ourselves that plays a role in our success. Surrendering to divine blessings involves recognising that our efforts are amplified and guided by a source beyond our human capacity.

As the narrator of this journey, I am not merely a son or a co-heir with Jesus Christ but also a servant—a humble advocate for spiritual alignment in business. I want you to consider involving God in your auto brokerage venture or any venture. This isn't an imposition but an invitation to explore a dimension beyond the tangible forces at play.

Acknowledging the formidable forces at work in the business world, this step proposes the concept of Kingdom business—conducting business for God. In this paradigm, you are not just an entrepreneur; you become an employee of the Supreme Being, the Creator of the universe. It's an alignment that helps you transcend worldly challenges and tap into divine guidance.

Whether or not you subscribe to a specific faith, involving spiritual principles in your business is not about imposing religious beliefs. It's an invitation to consider universal values of integrity, compassion, and a higher purpose transcending the material realm. Embracing Kingdom principles is an acknowledgement of a broader perspective in pursuing success.

QUESTIONS AND REFLECTIONS

1. The chapter highlights the need for early commitment and strategic focus to pursue excellence in auto brokerage. How do you approach strategic planning and commitment when embarking on a new endeavour?
2. Explore delivering quality service for lasting impact beyond mere financial gains. How do you envision the effect of providing exceptional service in the auto brokerage industry, both for clients and for your professional fulfilment?
3. The chapter discusses the importance of networking dynamics and professionalism from the outset. How do you plan to incorporate these principles into your journey towards becoming a successful auto broker?
4. How do you perceive the integration of spiritual principles into business practices, and what potential benefits do you foresee in adopting such an approach?

Chapter 3: Knowledge of Car Types – A Fundamental Exploration

The diversity of car types mirrors the evolving societal mindset at the collective and individual levels. In this era of rapid technological advancements, the ability to transform ideas into reality is more prevalent than ever. Companies are introducing cars of various shapes and sizes, emphasising the need for a foundational understanding of these diverse vehicle types.

Below, you'll discover a glimpse of these car varieties. Harness this knowledge and leverage it according to your inspiration. Embrace the season of innovation—it's yours to explore.

SEDAN

A sedan has four doors and a traditional trunk. Like vehicles in many categories, they are available in a range of sizes, from small (subcompact vehicles like Nissan Versa and Kia Rio) to compacts (Honda Civic, Toyota Corolla), mid-size (Honda Accord, Nissan Altima), and full-size (Toyota Avalon, Dodge Charger). Luxury brands like Mercedes-Benz and Lexus have sedans in similar sizes as well.

Simply put, a sedan is a 4-door passenger with a trunk separate from the passengers with a three-box body; that is, the engine, the area for passengers, and the trunk.

COUPE

A coupe has historically been considered a two-door car with a trunk and a solid roof. This would include cars like a Ford Mustang or Audi A5 or two-seat sports cars like the Chevrolet Corvette or the Porsche Boxster. Recently, however, car companies have started to apply the word "coupe" to four-door cars or crossovers with low, sleek rooflines that they deem "coupe-like." This includes vehicles such as a Mercedes Benz CLS sedan and a BMW X6 SUV. At Car and Driver, we still consider a coupe to be a two-door car.

SPORTS CAR

These are the sportiest, hottest, coolest-looking coupes and convertibles—low to Aston Martin Vantage he ground, sleek, and often expensive. They generally are two-seaters but sometimes have small rear seats as well. Cars like the Porsche 911 and Mazda Miata are typical sports cars, but you can stretch the definition to include muscle cars like the Ford Mustang and Dodge Challenger. Then there are the high-end exotic dream cars with sky-high price tags for the one percent, like the Ferrari 488 GTB and Aston Martin Vantage, which stop traffic with their spaceship looks.

STATION WAGON

Wagons are similar to sedans but have an extended roofline and a hatch door at the rear instead of a trunk. Some, like the Subaru Outback or Audi A4 Allroad, have elevated ground clearance and rugged body cladding to make them more like a sport-utility vehicle (SUV). Still, they are nonetheless closely related to sedans. Wagons have fallen from favour during the past few decades, and relatively few are available for sale.

HATCHBACK

Traditionally, the term "hatchback" has meant a compact or subcompact sedan with a squared-off roof and a rear flip-up hatch door that provides access to the vehicle's cargo area instead of a conventional trunk. The Volkswagen Golf and Kia Rio are two typical hatchbacks. More recently, rear hatches have found their way onto larger cars, like the Audi A7 and Kia Stinger. They look like sedans, but they actually have a steeply raked hatchback that affords easier accessibility to the cargo area and greater carrying capacity than a traditional trunk would.

SPORT-UTILITY VEHICLE (SUV)

SUVs—tend to be taller and boxier than sedans, offer an elevated seating position, and have more ground clearance than a car. They include a station wagon-like cargo area that is accessed through a flip-up rear hatch door, and many offer all-wheel drive. The larger ones have three rows of seats. Luxury brands offer many SUV models in most of the same size categories. There is no generally accepted definition of an SUV, but it's good to at least know the basic features of an SUV: high-capacity engine, all-wheel drive, high ground clearance, longer wheelbase, somewhat box-like body, and high seating position.

MINIVAN

Minivans are the workhorses of the family car world, the best at carrying people and cargo in an efficient package. They're called minivans, but they are far from "mini." That's because they are tall boxes-on-wheels with sliding side doors for easy access and a rear hatch that opens to a large cargo area. Most minivans have adjustable seats in their second and third rows that often can be removed or even folded into the floor to create a huge open cargo bay. The Honda Odyssey and Chrysler Pacifica are great examples of the breed.

Microcars

These are tiny cars that often come with an engine size of less than one litre and 700c. They come in various unusual designs and are ideal for city traffic due to their fuel efficiency and parking ease.

The microcar is most often a two-passenger vehicle. Examples of microcars include cyclecars, bubble cars, and the Tata Nano car. Modern microcars are most often electrically powered.

CUV (Crossover)

A crossover is often confused with an SUV. The crossover is a light off-road car with some SUV features. A crossover often comes with a two-wheel drive but can also come with 4-wheel-drive. It is basically an off-road car chassis but more built for city traffic. A key differentiating factor is the chassis – the crossover uses a light monochrome while the SUV utilises a ladder frame chassis. Basically, it means that a CUV shares the frame of a car, and the SUV shares the frame of a truck. It can often be referred to as a mix of an SUV and a hatchback.

Roadster

A roadster car is basically a cabriolet car with two doors and often does not have a backseat. They are, therefore, good for only two people. When it comes to size, they are often very small. They often have a sporty look and are perfect for those who enjoy good weather with their friend or fiancée.

Van

A Van is a two or three-seater car model that is often used to transport goods. They often have a sealed cabin from the cargo area, and they often do not have windows to the cargo area, but some models have glass windows at the rear doors for passengers.

Supercars

These are high-performance cars with large engines. Most are two-seaters while being very expensive; some are going for as much as one million dollars. Most have V8 or V12 while generating over 500 hp. Depending on the model, the supercar often comes with an open roof.

Luxury Cars

A luxury car is exactly what it sounds like – luxury. They are often very expensive and have all the latest functions for a comfortable ride. They often have a very powerful engine, but not very fast in corners and at race tracks. This is because they often have so many functions for comfort, so they are usually very heavy.

A luxury car can also be a supercar or sports car and the definition is often referred to very expensive cars with great comfort.

Muscle Cars

Muscle cars are cars with big muscles under the hood. Muscle cars are often referred to as older American cars with very large and powerful engines, but muscle cars also exist in modern cars. Muscle cars are usually not that fast at race tracks around corners, but when going in a straight line, like drag racing, not many other cars can beat them. Ford Mustang and Dodge Challenger are two very typical cars when it comes to muscle cars.

Mini Trucks

A mini truck is precisely what it sounds like – a small truck, and it is a mix of a Pickup truck and a truck. They often have two or three seats and an open cargo area but can also come with a closed area. They are often built on a truck chassis and are often pretty strong built for heavy loading.

Cabriolet

These car models come with a retractable roof. They can both be two-seaters or four-seaters. They can basically be any car model with a retractable roof, while the roadster is often a special car model.

Limousine

A limousine is a stretched car that is often used by celebrities and pop stars. It features an elongated base and can be created from various car models. They are often not created like this in the factories but are rebuilt after leaving the factory, often by special companies.

Truck

In this place on the list, you find the truck. While they are not really a car type, they can come in many forms and are still a vehicle type, so we wanted to include it. Most people know what a truck is. It is a two- or three-seater vehicle type, sometimes equipped with a bed behind the seats. It has a large cargo area and is primarily used for transporting goods by companies.

PICKUP TRUCK

A pickup truck has a passenger cab and an open cargo bed in the rear. Virtually all pickups offer some form of all-wheel drive or part-time four-wheel drive—the latter for off-road use only. With one exception—the mid-sized Honda Ridgeline —pickup bodies are cabs mounted to a separate steel frame. The Ridgeline is more like a crossover with the rear section of the roof lopped off to expose a cargo bed. Currently, pickup trucks come in two size categories: full-size and mid-size.

Bus

A bus is a large motor vehicle carrying passengers by road, typically one serving the public on a fixed route and for a fare.

Buses may be used for scheduled bus transport, scheduled coach transport, school transport, private hire, or tourism; promotional buses may be used for political campaigns and others are privately operated for a wide range of purposes, including rock and pop band tour.

QUESTIONS AND REFLECTIONS

1. After reading about the various types of cars, which categories do you find most interesting or relevant to your potential clients in the auto brokerage business? Why?

2. How do you think advancements in technology and shifting consumer preferences have influenced the evolution of car types over the years? Consider how factors like environmental concerns, urbanization, and lifestyle changes may impact future trends.

3. As an auto broker, how important is it to stay updated on the latest trends and developments in the automotive industry? How might your knowledge of different car types help you better understand and cater to the needs and preferences of your clients?

4. Some auto brokers choose to specialize in specific types of cars, while others prefer to offer a wide range of options. What factors would you consider when deciding whether to specialize or generalize in your auto brokerage business?

5. Some auto brokers choose to specialize in specific types of cars, while others prefer to offer a wide range of options. What factors would you consider when deciding whether to specialize or generalize in your auto brokerage business?

6. How do you envision using your knowledge of car types to educate and empower your clients in making informed purchasing decisions? Consider how you might tailor your approach based on factors like budget, lifestyle, and personal preferences.

7. As an auto broker, how would you navigate ethical considerations related to recommending specific car types to clients? What steps would you take to ensure transparency and integrity in your interactions?

8. Reflect on the importance of continuous learning and staying updated on new developments in the automotive industry. How do you plan to incorporate ongoing education and professional development into your journey as an auto broker?

9. Finally, take a moment to reflect on your own experiences and interests related to cars. How does your personal passion or expertise align with the knowledge and insights gained from this chapter? How might you leverage your unique perspective to differentiate yourself in the auto brokerage market?

Chapter 4: Knowledge of Car Brands

From my extensive knowledge of car brands spanning various continents and countries, it's evident that China, particularly in Asia, leads in automotive innovations globally. Understanding the dynamics of the automotive industry is integral to my confidence, whether operating as a car salesperson or serving as an independent automotive business consultant, a broader term encapsulating the role of an auto broker.

My professional journey has seen me evolve from roles like fixing GPS trackers to being a car dealer and auto broker, reflecting the transient nature of expertise. I've discovered my niche as a business consultant for specific sectors through failures and successes. My mission is to empower individuals and businesses, providing insights, identifying challenges, and offering strategic pathways for growth and scalability.

This trajectory is rooted in accumulated knowledge rather than mere passion. Continuously building on this knowledge is not just about staying relevant; it's a commitment to transforming passion and the desire to contribute value into tangible outcomes for the broader community. I encourage you to explore the intricacies of car brands—learning about their origins, inspirations, survival stories, operational halts, and more. The wealth of knowledge in this domain is vast and incredibly enriching.

Car Brand	Active Years	Logo	Country
9ff	2001-present		German
Abadal	1912-1923		Spanish
Abarth	1949-present		Italian
Abbott-Detroit	1909-1919		American
ABT	1896-present		German
AC	1901-present		British
Acura	1986-present		Japanese

Aixam	1983-present	AIXAM	French
Alfa Romeo	1910-present		Italian
Alpina	1965-present		German
Alpine	1955-present		French
Alta	1962-1978	ALTA	Greek
Alvis	1919-1967	ALVIS	British
AMC	1954-1958	American Motors	American
Apollo	2004-present		German
Arash	1999-present		British
Arcfox	2017-present	ARCFOX	Chinese
Ariel	2001-present		British
ARO	1957-2006	aro	Romanian
Arrinera	2008-present		Polish
Arrival	2015-present	ARRIVAL	British
Artega	2006-present	Artega	Germany
Askam	1964-2015	ASKAM	Turkish

Aspark	2005-present		Japanese
Aston Martin	1913-present		British
Atalanta	2011-present	ATALANTA MOTORS	British
Auburn	1900-1937	AUBURN	American
Audi	1909-present		German
Audi Sport	1983-present	Audi Sport	German
Austin	1905-1952	Austin	British
Autobacs	1947-present	AUTOBACS	Japanese
Autobianchi	1955-1995		Italian
Axon	2005-present	Axon	British
BAC	2009-present		British
BAIC Motor	2010-present	北京汽车 BAIC MOTOR	Chinese
Baojun	2010-present	宝骏汽车	Chinese
BeiBen	1988-present		Chinese
Bentley	1919-present		British
Berkeley	1956-1960		British

Berliet	1899-1978		French
Bertone	1912-2014		Italian
Bestune	2006-present		Chinese
BharatBenz	2011-present		Indian
Birkin Cars	1982-present		South African
Bitter	1971-present		German
Bizzarrini	1964-1969		Italian
BMW	1916-present		German
BMW M	1972-present		German
Borgward	1919-present		German
Bowler	1985-present		British
Brabus	1977-present		German
Brammo	2002-present		American
Brilliance	2002-present		Chinese
Bristol	1945-present		British
Brooke	2002-present		British
Bufori	1986-present		Malaysian
Bugatti	1909-present		French

Buick	1903-present		American
BYD	1995-present		Chinese
Byton	2016-present		Chinese
Cadillac	1902-present		American
CAMC	1999-present		Chinese
Canoo	2017-present		American
Caparo	2006-present		British
Carlsson	1989-present		German
Caterham	1973-present		British
Changan	1962-present		Chinese
Changfeng	1950-present		Chinese
Chery	1997-present		Chinese
Chevrolet	1911-present		American
Chevrolet Corvette	1953-present		American
Chrysler	1925-present		American
Cistalia	1946-1963		Italian
Citroën	1919-present		French
Cizeta	1988-1994		American
Cole	1909-1925		American

Corre La Licorne	1901-1949		French
Dacia	1966-present	DACIA	Romanian
Daewoo	1982-2002		South Korean
DAF	1993-present	DAF A PACCAR COMPANY	Dutch
Daimler	1886-present	DAIMLER	German
Dartz	2009-present		Latvian
Datsun	1931-present	DATSUN	Japanese
David Brown	2013-present	DAVID BROWN	British
Dayun	1987-present		Chinese
De Tomaso	1959-2015		Argentine Italian
Delage	1905-1953	DELAGE	French
DeLorean	1975-1982	DMC	American
Desoto	1928-1961	DESOTO	American
Detroit Electric	1907-1939		American
Devel Sixteen	2013-present		Emiratis
Diahatsu	1907-present		Japanese
Diatto	1905-1929	DIATTO	Italian
DINA	1951-present	DINA	Mexican
DKW	1916-1966	DKW	German

Dodge	1900-present		American
Dodge Viper	1992-present	DODGE	American
Donfeng	1969-present	东风汽车公司 DONGFENG MOTOR CORPORATION	Chinese
Donkervoot	1978-present	DONKERVOORT	Dutch
Drako Motors	2013-present	DRAKO	American
DS	2009-present		French
Duesenberg	1913-1937	DUESENBERG 8	American
Eagle	1988-1999		American
EDAG	1969-present	EDAG	German
Edsel	1957-1960		American
Eicher	1948-present		Indian
Elemental	2012-present	ELEMENTAL	Britain
Elfin	1957-present		Australian
Elva	1955-present	ELVA	British
Englon	2010-2013		Chinese
ERF	1933-2007	ERF	British
Eterniti	2010-2014		British
Exeed	2017-present	EXEED	Chinese
Facel Vega	1939-1964		French

Faraday Future	2014-present		American
FAW	1953-present		Chinese
FAW Jiefang	2003-present		Chinese
Ferrari	1947-present		Italian
Fiat	1899-present		Italian
Fioravanti	1987-present		Italian
Fisker	2007-2014		American
Foden	1887-2006		British
Force	1958-present		Indian
Ford	1903-present		American
Ford Mustang	1964-present		American
Foton	1996-present		Chinese
FPV	2002-2014		Australian
Franklin	1902-1934		American
Freightliner	1942-present		American
GAC Group	1997-present		Chinese
Gardner Douglas	1990-present		British
GAZ	1932-present		Russian

Geely	1986-present		Chinese
General Motors	1908-present		American
Genesis	2015-present		South Korean
Geo	1989-1997		American
Geometry	2019-present		Chinese
Gilbern	1957-1973		Walsh
Gillet	1992-present		Belgian
Ginetta	1958-present		British
GMC	1911-present		American
Golden Dragon	1992-present		Chinese
Gonow	2003-present		Chinese
Greatwall	1984-present		Chinese
Grinall	1991-present		British
Hafei	1980-2022		Chinese
Haima	1992-present		Chinese
Haval	2013-present		Chinese
Hawtai	2000-present		Chinese
Hennessey	1991-present		United States
Higer	1998-present		Chinese
Hilman	1907-1931		British

Hindustan Motors	1942-present	HM Hindustan Motors	Indian
Hino	1942-present		Japanese
Hispano-Suiza	1904-1968		Spanish
Holden	1856-present		Australian
Hommell	1990-2003		French
Honda	1948-present		Japanese
Hongqi	1958-present		Chinese
Hongyan	2003-present		Chinese
Horch	1904-1932		German
HSV	1987-present		Australian
Hudson	1909-1954		American
Hummer	1992-2010	HUMMER	American
Hupmobile	1909-1940	Hupmobile	American
Hyundai	1967-present		South Korean
IC Bus	2002-present		American
IH	1902-1985		American
IKCO	1962-present	IKCO	Iranian
Infiniti	1989-present		Japanese
Innocenti	1947-1997		Italian

Intermeccanica	1959-present		Italian
International	1902-present		American
Irizar	1889-present		Spanish
Isdera	1969-present		German
Iso	1953-1974		Italian
Isuzu	1934-present		Japanese
Iveco	1975-present		Italian
IVM	2007-present		Nigerian
JAC	1964-present		Chinese
Jaguar	1922-present		British
Jawa	1929-present		Czech
JBA Motors	1982-present		British
Jeep	1941-present		American
Jensen	1934-1976		British
Jetta	2019-present		Chinese
JMC	1968-present		Chinese
Kaiser	1945-1953		American
Kamaz	1969-present		Russian
Kantanka Automobile	1994-present		Kenyan

Karlmann King	2017-present		Italian American
Karma	2015-present		American
Keating	2006-present		British
Kenworth	1912-present		American
Kia	1944-present		South Korean
Kiira Motors	2014-present		Ugandan
King Long	1988-present		Chinese
Koenigsegg	1994-present		Swedish
KTM	1934-present		Austrian
Lada	1966-present		Russian
Lagonda	1906-present		British
Lamborghini	1963-present		Italian
Lancia	1906-present		Italian
Land Rover	1948-present		British
Landwind	2002-present		Chinese
Laraki	1999-present		Moroccan
LEVC	2013-present		British
Lexus	1983-present		Japanese

Leyland	1896-1968		British
Li Auto	2015-present		Chinese
Lifan	1992-present		Chinese
Ligier	1968-present		France
Lincoln	1917-present		American
Lister	1954-present		British
Lloyd	1908-1963		German
Lobini	1999-present		Brazilian
Lordstown	2018-present		American
Lotus	1952-present		British
Lucid	1992-2010		American
Luxgen	2009-present		Taiwanese
Lynk & Co	2016-present		Chinese-Swedish
Mack	1900-present		American
Mahindra	1945-present		Indian
MAN	1758-present		German
Mansory	1989-present		German
Marlin	1979-present		British
Mastretta	1987-present		Mexican
Maxus	2011-present		Chinese

Maybach	1909-present		German
MAZ	1944-present		Belarusian
Mazda	1920-present		Japanese
Mazzanti	2002-present		Italian
McLaren	1963-present		British
Melkus	1959-present		German
Mercedes Benz	1926-present		German
Mercedes-AMG	1967-present		German
Mercury	1938-2011		American
Merkur	1984-1989		American
MEV	2003-present		British
MG	1924-present		British
Microcar	1984-2008		French
Mini	1959-present		British
Mitsouka	1968-present		Japanese
Mitsubishi	1970-present		Japanese
MK	1996-present		British
Mobius Motors	2010-present		Kenyan

Morgan	1910-present	MORGAN	Chinese
Morris	1919-1984		British
Mosler	1985-2013	MOSLER	American
Navistar	1993-present	NAVISTAR	American
NEVS	2012-present	NEVS	Swedish
Nikola	2014-present	NIKOLA	American
NIO	2014-present	NIO	Chinese
Nissan	1933-present	NISSAN	Japanese
Nissan GT-R	2007-present	GT R	Japanese
Nissan Nismo	1984-present	nismo	Japanese
Noble	1999-present	NOBLE	British
Nord	2018-present	NORD	Nigerian
Oltcit	1976-1991		Romanian
Opel	1862-present		German
OSCA	1947-1967		Italian
Paccar	1905-present	PACCAR	American
Packard	1899-1958		American
Pagani	1992-present	PAGANI	Italian
Panhard	1887-2012	PL	French

Panoz	1989-present		American
Pegaso	1946-1994		Spanish
Perodua	1993-present		Malaysian
Peterbilt	1939-present		American
Peugeot	1896-present		French
PGO	1985-present		French
Pierce-Arrow	1901-1938		American
Pininfarina	1930-present		Italian
Plymouth	1928-2001		American
Polestar	1996-present		Swedish
Pontiac	1926-2010		American
Porsche	1931-present		German
Praga	1907-present		Czech
Premier	1944-2001		Indian
Prodrive	1984-present		British
Proton	1983-present		Malaysian
Qoros	2007-present		Chinese
Radical	1997-present		British
RAM	2010-present		American

Rambler	1900-1983		American
Ranz	2013-present		
Renault	1899-present		French
Renault Samsung	1994-present		South Korean
Rezvani	2014-present		Iranian American
Riley	1913-1969		British
Rimac	2009-present		Croatian
Rinspeed	1979-present		Swiss
Rivian	2009-present		American
Roewe	2006-present		Chinese
Rolls-Royce	1906-present		British
Ronart	1984-present		British
Rossion	2006-present		American
Rover	1878-2005		British
RUF	1939-present		German
Saab	1937-present		Swedish
SAIC Motor	1955-present		Chinese
Saipa	1965-present		Iranian
Saleen	1984-present		American

Saturn	1985-2010		American
Scania	1891-present		Swedish
Scion	2003-2016		Japanese
SEAT	1950-present		Spanish
Setra	1951-present		German
Shacman	1968-present		Chinese
Simca	1934-1970		French
Singer	1875-1970		British
Singulato	2014-present		Chinese
Sinotruk (CNHTC)	1935-present		Chinese
Sisu	1931-present		Finish
Škoda	1895-present		Czech
Smart	1994-present		German
Soueast	1995-present		Chinese
Spania GTA	1994-present		Spanish
Spyker	1898-present		Dutch
SsanYong	1954-present		South Korean
SSC	1998-present		American
Sterling	1906-2008		American

Studebaker	1852-1967		American
Stutz	1911-1939		American
Subaru	1953-present		Japanese
Suffolk	1922-1935		British
Suzuki	1909-present		Japanese
Talbot	1903-1994		British
Tata	1946-present		Indian
Tatra	1850-present		Czech
Tauro Sport Auto	2010-present		Spanish
TechArt	1987-present		German
Tesla	2003-present		American
Toyota	1937-present		Japanese
Toyota Alphard	2002-present		Japanese
Toyota Century	1967-present		Japanese
Toyota Crown	1955-present		Japanese
Tramontana	2007-present		Spanish
Trion	2012-present		American

Triumph	1885-1984		British
Troller	1995-present		Brazilian
Tucker	1944-1950		American
TVR	1947-present		British
UAZ	1941-present		Russian
UD	1935-present		Japanese
Ultima	1992-present		British
Vandenbrink	2006-present		Dutch
Vauxhall	1857-present		British
Vector	1971-present		American
Vencer	2010-present		Dutch
Venturi	1984-present		French
Venucia	2010-present		Chinese
VinFast	2017-present		Vietnamese
VLF	1965-present		American
Volkswagen	1937-present		German
Volvo	1927-present		Swedish
W Motors	2012-present		Emiratis
Wallyscar	2006-present		Tunisian

Wanderer	1896-1945		German
Wartbug	1955-1991		German
Weltmeister	2015-present		Chinese
Western Star	1967-present		American
Westfield	1982-present		British
WEY	2016-present		Chinese
Wiesmann	1988-present		German
Willys-Overland	1908-1963		American
Workhorse	1998-present		American
Wuling	1982-present		Chinese
XPeng	2014-present		Chinese
Yulon	1953-present		Chinese
Yutong	1963-present		Chinese
Zarooq Motors	2014-present		Emiratis
Zastava	2000-present		Serbian
Zaz	1923-present		Ukrainian
Zenos	2012-present		British
Zenvo	2009-present		Danish
Zhongtong	1958-present		Chinese
Zinoro	2013-present		Chinese

Zotye	2003-present	众泰汽车 ZOTYE AUTO	Chinese

QUESTIONS AND REFLECTIONS

1. Reflect on the diversity of car brands listed and how they represent the global automotive landscape. What patterns or trends do you notice in terms of the distribution of brands across different regions?

2. Many car brands listed have a rich history dating back decades or even centuries. How do you think the historical legacy of a brand influences its reputation and perception in the market today?

3. In such a competitive industry, innovation and adaptation are key to a brand's success. Can you identify any car brands that have demonstrated particularly innovative or adaptive strategies to stay relevant in the market?

4. Among the list of car brands, are there any relatively new or lesser-known brands that you believe have the potential to become major players in the future? What factors contribute to their potential success?

5. Many consumers exhibit strong loyalty to certain car brands. What do you think drives this brand loyalty, and how do car brands cultivate and nurture it over time?

6. Reflect on the dynamic nature of the automotive market and how factors such as technological advancements, regulatory changes, and shifting consumer preferences impact the success and sustainability of car brands.

7. Based on your reflections on the diverse landscape of car brands, what are your predictions for the future of the automotive industry? How do you envision the roles of established brands versus newer entrants shaping the industry's trajectory?

Chapter 5: Entrepreneurial Ideas in the Transportation Industry

The purpose of this chapter is to state a few commercial uses for some car types. As much as we have car lovers, we also have people looking to get into the auto business or any business that requires the use of vehicles. This chapter will give you new ideas and aid in building some of the ones you already have in mind.

Apart from being a car dealer or an auto broker, there are quite a few business opportunities one could take advantage of and become a master in.

Here are some commercial uses for some car types:

1. **Transportation businesses**: if you permit me to explain, I will mention a few transportation businesses you could use your vehicle for.

    a. Car-hire/rental services: You could rent out your vehicle for hire services or start a company that rents vehicles (which must be in good condition, though) for short periods for a fee. This business is profitable in cities and towns, as dignitaries in your country could hire your vehicle. Many may want to refrain from using their cars or official vehicles for functions or assignments. Many people and organisations are already running this business, so standing out and delivering quality service should be a priority for anyone looking to start this; lest I forget, employing responsible and professional drivers to drive your clients should also be included in your priority or must-do list. Sedans, SUVs, limousines, pickup trucks, luxury cars, and supercars suit this business.

    b. Ridesharing Platforms: Register your car with Uber, Lyft, or other platforms for a steady income stream. Alternatively, consider renting your vehicle to the platform for them to manage drivers and operations.

    c. Bridging the Gap: Imagine a service between public transportation and private cabs. Offer comfortable, clean hatchbacks, sedans, or station waggons for individuals seeking a more dignified and relaxed travel experience. Target working professionals, students, and those with limited mobility.

    d. You may rent your cars long-term to start-ups, organisations, and non-governmental organisations needing more funding to buy new or used vehicles.

2. **Beyond Passenger Transport**:

a. Ambulance Services: Cater to events, private companies, and the public with well-equipped vans, minivans, or station waggons. Partner with medical professionals and ensure proper licencing for this crucial service.

b. Farming Logistics: Assist farmers by transporting their produce from farms to markets or customers. Trucks, pickup trucks, and minivans are ideal, depending on the size and quantity of produce.

c. Delivery Delights: Become the go-to solution for transporting light and heavy goods. Serve e-commerce companies, manufacturers, individuals relocating, and those sending items across distances. Utilise a diverse fleet of trucks, vans, and minivans to cater to varied needs.

3. **Specialised Services, Maximum Profits**

   a. Unique Transportation: Carve a niche by specialising in transporting unusual items like modular houses, boat/aeroplane parts, refrigerated perishables, or medical supplies. High fees and limited clientele make this a lucrative option.

   b. Livestock Logistics: Assist farmers and animal owners in transporting livestock like cows, sheep, or horses. Choose suitable vehicles, like trucks and minivans, based on the size and number of animals.

   c. Caring for Seniors: Offer transportation services for senior citizens and the elderly. This socially responsible business caters to those needing driving licences, vehicles, or good eyesight. Consider a non-profit model if targeting low-income communities.

4. **Beyond the Vehicle**

   a. School & Staff Transportation: Provide reliable and safe transport for school children, company staff, or government personnel. Use buses, coaches, minibuses, or station waggons to ensure proper registration and licencing.

   b. Going the Extra Mile: Offer your services at airports, estates, universities, and even rock band tours. This diversifies your clientele and expands your reach.

Conclusion

A car is more than just a mode of personal transportation. It holds the potential for exciting commercial ventures. So, unleash your wheels, explore these possibilities, and carve your path to entrepreneurial success. Remember, the world awaits the manifestation of your ideas and who you truly are.

QUESTIONS AND REFLECTIONS

1. Reflect on the variety of entrepreneurial ideas presented in the transportation industry. Which ideas resonate with you the most, and why? Are there any particular business concepts that you find particularly innovative or intriguing?

2. As an auto broker, how can you introduce these diverse business ideas to clients interested in purchasing cars but need to be made aware of their various commercial opportunities? How can you educate and inspire them to consider alternative uses for their vehicles beyond personal transportation? How can auto brokers leverage their expertise and passion for cars to serve as enthusiasts and advocates for exploring these entrepreneurial avenues with their clients?

3. Finally, consider how these entrepreneurial ideas align with your interests, skills, and values. Do any of these ideas spark your entrepreneurial spirit? How might you adapt or innovate upon these concepts to create a business venture that reflects your unique vision and goals?

Made in the USA
Las Vegas, NV
04 September 2024